Ultimate Guide to
DOING BUSINESS

That Makes Money
ON FACEBOOK

By: Brian Ernest Hayward

Copyright © 2017 by Brian Ernest Hayward and Published by

Brian Hayward for Hayward House Publishing

Published by Hayward House and Big Book Box A Member of the Brian

Hayward Group

Library of Congress Cataloging-in-Publication Data

Hayward, Brian. TITLE=**Wedding**, Journaling for success in your life / Brian Hayward. p. cm.

F.Q.T. **FREE QUICK TIPS**

ISBN-13: 978-1981560820

ISBN-10: 1981560823

Self-control. 2. Self-management (Psychology) 3. Success. 4. Success in business.

Big Book Box Press books are available at special discounts for bulk purchases

in the U.S. by corporat io ns, institut io ns, and other organizat io ns . For more

information, please contact the Special Markets Department at the Big Book Box

Books Group, 4613 Lanier drive, 4th Floor, Savannah, Ga 31405,or call (912) 224-

7502, or visit us at:

https://www.amazon.com/Brian-Ernest-Hayward/e/B06XT464NM

AUTHOR BIOGRAPHY

Brian Ernest Hayward is a passionate Author and Inspirational Speaker, internationally known for his unwavering dedication to creating positive change through the power of words. From religious and success books, to adult coloring books and artist how-tos, his writings touch on over 400 different subjects.

Today, all of Brian's publications are sold worldwide across multiple formats (Paperback, Kindle, and Large Print) and are translated into 21 different languages. He has also participated in over 100 speaking engagements spanning over 38 states.

INTRODUCTION

 *I* was taught by my teacher, Pastor Bill Winston, this prayer. This

prayer has served me well, and in due time it will serve you well. *Father I come before you in Jesus name, thank you for the anointing that's on me and these lips of clay. I know that because of your blessing, I speak this word today with excellency, accuracy, and boldness.*

I thank you for thinking through my mind and speaking through my lips and this

word will come forth unhindered, and unchecked by any outside force. Now I give you the praise for it and I fully expect signs, wonders, and miracles to confirm your word preached in Jesus name, Amen! This is a book about the "new creation" God has made me through Christ Jesus. Be inspired as you read toward greatness and achievement.

<u>YOUR PORTION</u>

Another of My teachers is Pastor Dr. Uebert Angel. Dr Uebert Angel is a very good bible teacher. Check out his books very soon, if you have not already. He mentioned this verse in his book entitled: God's Get Rich Quick Scheme. He notes, "Thus saith the LORD, thy Redeemer, the Holy One of Israel; I am the LORD thy God which teacheth thee to profit, which leadeth thee by the way that thou shouldest go. Isaiah 48:17 Do you see that, he teaches you to profit, by his word, by his spiritual laws, he wants to lead you the way you should go and that way is not into a financial wilderness, it's to take you to a place of the overflow for Jesus came so that you should have life and have it abundantly.

Lack is not your portion, sickness is not your portion, poverty is not your portion, and generational curses are not your portion.Work towards a seed, find good ground, sow your seed and act upon what you have sowed for, you will surely come back with a testimony.

MAKE THIS CONFESSION BEFORE READING THIS BOOK

MAKE THIS FULL CONFESSION EACH NIGHT FOR THE NEXT 30 DAYS. "I am a winner. I am blessed coming by in and blessed going out. I am blessed in all my efforts. I am blessed in all my undertakings. I am blessed even when I merely try. God's grace gives me greater victories even when I start later than others. Everything I put my hands to is blessed. Everything I show interest in acquiring, I am blessed with achieving. My mind is blessed in everything I think of. My ideas are blessed. My ideas are blessed with heavenly creativity. God prepared my deliverance before the foundation of the earth and he has already made all crooked places straight and opened doors that men have said are impossible to open. I am blessed with God's word

I keep sound wisdom and discretion. Wisdom resides in my heart and knowledge is pleasant to my soul. Discretion preserves me. Understanding keeps me and delivers me from all evil. My ways are ways of pleasantness and all my paths are peace. Thank You, Father, I always find wisdom for she says, "I love them that love me; And those that seek me early shall find me." I trust in the Lord with all my heart, and lean not to my own understanding.

I am born of incorruptible seed; And I walk and live by faith. Wisdom leads me when I go; keeps me when I sleep, and speaks with me when I wake. I refuse to accept any lies from the devil. The Holy Spirit is my Teacher, and guides me into all truth.

Contents

Introduction

The internet is all abuzz with Facebook and these days everyone is making a beeline for creating their own profile. On the whole, any online social networking website like Facebook has very quickly emerged as an astonishing stage to make pots of money online. With this e-book you will get exclusive information and secrets to earn thousands of dollars every month. All of this can be done without putting in a great deal effort and with zero investment.

As you keep reading this e-book and browse through each chapter, you will get an in-depth description of hidden secrets. You will get to know how this entire system can work in your favor. Here you would also see that each chapter or article is interwoven with others. This happens because attempts to repeat content have been avoided. Apart from this, correlating the different components of this e-book was vital to get comprehensive knowledge about Facebook. Start minting money by using Facebook and enjoy the array of marketing tips, business ideas and other suggestions. These suggestions and tips will be very useful in each chapter.

There are a lot of online marketers who have already used Facebook and have converted their business goals into huge success stories. These are the people who can make six figure incomes, in spite of very few working hours or when they go out for a vacation. One of the best advantages of this e-book is that you are not doing anything that is difficult or impossible. Through Facebook, you will just make sure that your business is more advertised and you are better informed than most others. Take the advantage of this knowledge and experience. Enjoy the exclusive elite class business clientele on Facebook by following the simple guidelines. These are enumerated and elaborated in the following chapters.

There have been a lot of social networking communities that have come and gone. Some were able to make their presence felt online for some years and then fell, while the others did not manage to make a mark, at all. However, but among them all, Facebook has emerged as a unique and exceptional concept. The simple reason behind this is the user friendly functioning of Facebook. The tools used here are extremely unsophisticated and the site follows a straightforward method where the users interface with each other. It has formidable speed, which is much higher compared to other social networking websites. Hence, Facebook has emerged as a huge winner on the social networking market.

Now it is time for you to take the lead using Facebook. You can get your business recognized with ease. The Facebook website ensures that your business becomes matchless. Since it is very easy to use, you can connect much faster with thousands of people. Out of these there are a lot of them who can be very beneficial to your business activities. You may have tried and given up on the Facebook approach earlier. But through the secrets given in this e-book you can get success like never before. The other social networking communities will not be able to create this experience for you. Facebook will aid you pave your way to success.

Why join Facebook?

With so many social networking sites around, you may be wondering why Facebook? Well, Facebook is actually a fad for in the generation Z. Those who are hip and trendy do have a Facebook account. The statistics and researches show that Facebook has become the largest social networking site in the world today. Millions have their account here on Facebook. The teenagers, adults and even the elderly love connecting with Facebook.

This turns out to be a fun method of reuniting with friends or family members with whom you may have lost touch or not spoken to for a long time already. This is also an ideal method of getting in touch with new friends. So, you can probably meet a new face or someone who can become your best friend or you eventually fell in love with.

Then there are a lot of cool Facebook applications that make networking so much fun. Out here you can get intellectual quizzes to tickle your funny bones or play games that you get addicted to. The games like Farmville here are some of the most popular ones.

Some of the other applications that you might enjoy here are opining. Those who are introverts can enjoy letting out their opinions and ideas. So Facebook is like an outlet through which you can express your self and give suggestions. This is one of the easiest social networking sites present today. Get an email to get started with your accounting procedure on Facebook.

Some of the necessary and vital information here is the email address. Once you have an account, you can start talking and networking with so many people. To expand any business, you need the right networking channel. Doing so helps to get you more business. For example, if you have an online store then a simple posting on your wall will bring the store to the notice of thousands. With this simple clicking, you can actually increase the number of individuals who are visiting your website.

Apart from this, Facebook offers a unique and cool tool to re-bond with old pals, classmates, relatives and even neighbors. You can now get in touch with long child sweethearts and old friends. Facebook is the latest fad for the current generation and through your Facebook status you can communicate with others. There are a lot of other things that one can do with their Facebook account apart from business and networking. It is expressing and giving you a new avatar.

Now you don't have to think twice about expressing what you feel. You can have debates with friends, suggest entertaining ideas or discuss about the current political scenario. On the whole, you learn more and are also able to help others learn more. The growth of the mind through Facebook is a factor that a lot of people overlook. Get a Facebook account now, for giving your business a makeover, making friends and of course, giving yourself a much needed channel of expression.

Marketing tips and ideas for Facebook

When the 90's introduced Friendster, it turned out to be one of the most popular things. A lot of people had an account here and almost anyone could create one here. This was an innovative and unique way of staying connected with friends. And since it is in the World Wide Web, it is easily accessible by people around the world. However, as they say that all good things have to come to an end. But the loss of one such website led to the creation of Facebook.

People forgot other social networking websites with the advent of Facebook. This is actually a very sophisticated mechanism of networking and advertising. Over here you can get connected with many business minded people. They have seen the potential of this website as a marketing tool. Once you have friends and social contacts on your list, it becomes very easy to increase and expand your business.

There are a lot of marketing gimmicks and tips that you can apply here. For example, if you have the flexibility to add friends of your choice, you can avoid adding a business contact or friend to your list, by denying their request. Choosing your own friends here is a big advantage. The Facebook user gets a message from the individual who has sent the request to be added. If confirmed, they will get the confirmation from the website. The message either invites such users to buy a certain product. For example, if the person you just added is a real estate agent then you can get their latest promotion.

It is quite simple and ethical to market your products on Facebook. As long as you are following this etiquette and marketing tips, you are bound to get success here. The first factor to keep in mind is that you have to write a message to the individual added to your list for expanding or widening business contacts. So you should reply with a thank you and give them the time for introducing the particular range of products and services.

Like with other business advertising techniques, Facebook is against hard selling. There is no doubt that it can become irritating for a probable customer to get forced into buying products or investing in services that they are not interested in. Introduce yourself first if you plan to send messages to your customers.

A lot of marketing tips are listed on the website itself. The process begins with your profile status and this should be kept as sincere as possible. Those who trust your product would be showing some levels of enthusiasm based on the info provided in the profile status. Don't patronize yourself but let the product details do the trick for you.

Start off by creating a business profile on Facebook

The first question that you must ask yourself here is 'How do I create a Facebook profile'. Well in this cyber technology era, the tools of communication take a different course. Those who are using only the telephone for distant communication should know that they are living in the caveman or dark ages. With the internet's introduction, people have been able to get in touch with others across the different continents. Get in touch with friends and loved ones in any corner of the world.

The growth of social networking sites like Facebook has made it easier to get instant updates. You can know all that is happening around you and the world in a matter of seconds. The other factor here is that these famous social networking sites can help you create profiles with ease. These are not regular profiles, but are a summary of what you are, what your business is all about and other relevant factors.

The first prerequisite here is to have an email address. Anyone with an email address can create a Facebook profile. However, there are age requirements on

Facebook that all the account users should adhere to. Some of these are being 13years. Even though this age requirement is not strictly followed, it is suggested that you abide by them. Not following the rules may result in cancellation of account.

Those who have a valid email address and abide by the other criteria can start doing business on Facebook instantly. The idea is that once you sign up for a Facebook account, you should give enough information to impress others. Not too much, but a little information would cover these requirements. There is some necessary information here which is compulsory. Apart from this you can give information to create an impact on the other users.

For example, if you have a business of garments then adding some facts about it can help others know about it. Once you submit these details, you will get the confirmation email from Facebook. At this email address you will have to click on a given link to ensure that your email address is valid. Double check your id before submitting the same or else you will have to repeat the ordeal again.

Once you log into your account, search for your friends and find relatives here. Those who are new to the social networking site should know that you can add business contacts here also.

Those who already have friends on this site can request them to add you on the list. This entire process can be repeated for finding other friends. The concept of adding friends is a major tool for staying connected. With friends you can get updated information about social activities and happenings on your Facebook account.

Other than this you would also be sharing your opinions, likes and dislikes and even other information. Add some pictures of yours here and create an album that you can share with your friends. The Facebook wall, you can post interesting status or simply update about what is going on in your life.

How to create a business page on Facebook?

The Social networking site "Facebook" is being used by more than 100 million people. It is a place to share information, find friends and obtain personal information regarding them.

If you are looking to find marketing potential, Facebook is one of the spreading networks all over the world. How to create a business page in Facebook? It is very easy, all you have to do is to browse and surf the internet and have a good study. Initially you must name your page, to help the customers recognize it, then upload Photos. It is mandatory to post or upload some pictures for your fans and customers as it makes the page more friendly and approachable. News Feeds will help you to search, browse, and find new businesses.

Make the account clear and easy as this would help friends and customers search through information without wasting much time, especially when you're adding Personal Information about yourself and your business. Underneath the profile picture, enter as much basic and detailed page of information as you can see.

Elaborating about the product and maximizing the details will help the customers gain a comprehensive knowledge about the same. Lastly publishing of the page and sharing it to the world is an absolute necessity. Like a contact listing on a cellular phone or website, the public profile of yours helps your customers to engage with other friends on your behalf.

After finishing the Business page, you must update it almost everyday, by uploading new pictures of your products, fresh photos, upcoming events and latest promotion. Facebook users are so much tangled with varied business pages that you need to attract them with every new aspect of your products, and also send an everyday update to fans.

You need to create presence that appears and acts like the user profiles of many other people. This can be used to connect and get in touch with new customers and amplify your advertisement on Facebook. A Facebook page helps to have a glimpse of the product which you or your friends are advertising. After creating a page, you must start to make a conversation. Stories that link to your pages on Facebook can go to other friends through modes like News Feed. As friends interact on the page, news will be broadcasted by your own news Feeds. This eventually spreads the network by bonding with different Facebook users.

Customer awareness has to be captured; you can spread your page even more via Facebook Advertisements. It can be promoted to a higher level by choosing your text, graphic and aim audience.

Business on Facebook

Facebook is not only confined to search friends and have those expressions articulated but it has become a platform which initiates business, advertising and good relation with the customers. Facebook has become part of the daily activity. Facebook accounts can be personal or you can have business dealings on it. It offers diverse applications that can be used both for personal enjoyment and business purposes. If you have set up your personal Facebook account, you can use it for business as well.

Facebook account users can conquer new avenues, and venture into small business using this social networking site, since it is easier for people to see you and your products here. There are millions of Facebook users around the world who can be potential customers. This becomes a platform for publicity of brands either new or existing ones. All it would need is uploading of some photos of the respective products. Tag these photos among friends and give details on how to order, pay and receive the items they have purchased. It is quite popular for people who are retailing or reselling because of the ease of access and it being very user friendly.

Facebook users have come to realize that this social networking site can be utilized as an efficient business tool without much of hassle. It provides free advertisement of your products. Aside from the fact that it has become more convenient for buyers to do online shopping, you can haggle with the price set by the seller as well. Nothing beats like shopping at the comfort of your own home while waiting for your crops to harvest.

Small businesses in Facebook have been sprouting like mushrooms. It creates an opportunity for small entrepreneurs to introduce their products using Facebook. It has become their test of water before plunging into a bigger venture, thus has become an avenue for potential world market.

The people on your social network list can help you in doing business on Facebook. You can ask them to share photos and information regarding your business to other people not included in your list. This will give your business a wider market. You will be able to cater to people of different ages, cultures and even nationalities.

Even the biggest names in business found this opportunity quite enterprising and expected good results. They use Facebook to advertise their company, their products and their latest promos as well. A Facebook account user needs to become a fan of a specific advertisement in order to gain full access of the account. And the good thing about this one is the friends of those who have access to your site will be able to see it as well.

Business on Facebook has a lot of potential to grow and prosper. All you need to do is to make your account as interesting as possible so that other Facebook account users will be enticed to check on what you have to offer. A good reputation of the product is sure to reap good result. Publicity among friends may help in judging the product. Thus, the business spreads and creates its own network with ease and promptness which is always desirable.

<u>Importance of creating a fan page on Facebook</u>

The main purpose of Facebook site is to keep all the friends and relatives connected. It has also opened the door for business owners, organizations and as well as political parties in promoting their advocacy and products. If the person has an account on the site and they want to become a fan of any other organization, they just have to become a fan of that particular organization.

As the popularity of the site is growing, it has become a major source through which the company and other institutions can advertise. The social network of Facebook is even used by the political parties for their campaign. If the person really thinks about this in detail, then they will see that it is the most efficient way to advertise their business. At the same time, the person also gets the privilege to get their business advertised free of cost. It is just that they should have the right knowledge of the trick that needs to be played for the free advertisement. The social networking site of Facebook is the best way in which a person gets to know what the public thinks about their business.

To make a fan page on Facebook can be tricky if the person is not familiar with the site. But the fact is that if the person knows how to make an account on Facebook and use it, it would be really easy to make a fan page on this site.

The things that need to be considered by the person who wants to make a fan page is that he/ she will have to define the business and its personality in such a way on the profile that the person looking at the ad gets impressed. The main aim of the ad is to get the person attracted to the organization so that they visit it and become a fan of it.

While the company makes sure that the content of the fan page is interesting, it is also important that they make sure that the photo that is uploaded on the page is attractive. At the same time the creator of the page can put a link on the page so that the person who visits the site is directly diverted to the website of the organization. They should make sure that the website is also very attractive. The main purpose of any organization is not to divert the traffic to the site but to generate business. This can only be possible if the person takes interest in the website. The creator of the fan page should never run out of ideas and should always work on the project to improve it so that the organization is successful.

If the organization has created a fan page on Facebook, then they can also send updates to their fans on the upcoming events. It is vital that the maximum people visit the fan page so that the company as well as the business grows.

Facebook helps the company in getting business

Facebook is a social networking site that also helps businesses to prosper. It also has the same traffic that one can find in Google. On the right side of the front page, there are many advertisements from different companies, organizations and groups.

A person who uses the internet has an account on Facebook. The people log in to the account on a daily basis. They don't have any special task to do on the site. It is just that they want to get some information from their friend or to use and enjoy the applications that are available on Facebook.

The companies who use the website for business purpose get a lot of exposure. However, there is a vast difference between the ads that get published on Facebook in comparison to the other search engines like Google, Yahoo and MSN. The major difference in the ad of Facebook is whenever it gets published or for that matter if anyone sees the ad they will also see a button below the same. If you feel that the advertisement which is published is the one you are looking for, then just click on the link. The button will show the sign of a thumb. You also have the privilege to unlike the ad at any point. At the same time if the person is interested in knowing more about the ad, he/ she can click on the link and they will get all the information on the service and the products in details.

It should also be kept in mind that if the person holds an account on Facebook, he/she gets the privilege to advertise their own business. The users who advertise their business should keep in mind to have a good website so that when the person clicks on the link they can get directly to the site of the business.

An ad on Facebook consists of 25 characters in the title and the copy gets the maximum of 135 characters. The creator should design their ad in such a manner that catches the eye of maximum users of Facebook. There should always be a target for the person who is publishing the advertisements. After the decision is made by the creator then he/ she can easily pay by using their plastic money.

The users of Facebook, who advertise the ad on the site also gets the privilege to change the ad at any point in time if they decide that they want to change the ad in order to get more clicks on their link. This is just like a test that one takes to promote the business.

It can be any site on the internet that advertises their business, but the main purpose of the creator of the ad should be to make an interesting title. After the person suffering the site finds that the ad is attractive, then only they will go and visit the site.

Making money on Facebook

Facebook releases a new platform and presents an exclusive break for the developers, marketers and business people in tapping the social network by the total active, viral and young crowd.

In the last few weeks, there has been increasing concern towards developers to reveal ways for monetizing their applications on Facebook. The pest of instantaneous online achievement is that you cannot maintain pricey servers to maintain hundreds or thousands or even millions of users on Facebook. A Question arises: how could developers make money using Facebook application? We cannot answer the question accurately, but our suggestions are listed below:

1. SELL: Developing an application solely and selling it to the interested parties. It was done previously in the same fashion, for example TextMe was purchased by Mozes'.

2. DEVELOP: Circuitous funds of source: developing application for third party under contract based. On Facebook's developers' forums, many companies' post number of contract jobs. The developers available for Facebook applications indicate a huge difference in supply and demand. This results in finding the potential clients and charging them with reasonable rates without any harass.

3. ADVERTISEMENT: Make use of advertisement, affiliate market and cross-promotion proposals. Facebook doesn't support JavaScript embedding, so there is no possibility of using Google Adsense. Adsense can be entrenched throughout iFrames; this is being popular with Facebook developers against Google TOS.

4. MICROPAYMENTS: During micro-payment dealings, services can be sold out within Facebook. The access to premium service PayPal can potentially defer

sensible income. This depends on the applications reason, size and other potential users.

5. <u>GETTING INVESTMENT:</u> When something is available in hand, it needs lacking the funds to scale it. For this, applying an investment through Bay partners and the others who have uttered interest in funding the applications for Facebook is required. This course is apt for a starter who is planning to enlarge world wide beyond and within Facebook.

Facebook actively maintains a vast community. It was noticed that the active users were over 29 million; about half logs in every day which is infrequency amongst Web 2.0 companies (comparing with Google Videos is about 3% users actively). If Facebook is successful convincing its users in shelling out $1 and send those silly essential imagery gifts to each other; for sure an intelligent developer or set up will find other options to earn money using Facebook applications without any involvement of obscuring in ads by their users.

Expand your business on Facebook

In an age of social media and Internet, new concepts and business avenues have come into view around the world and assisting people to start new businesses and find simple solutions for their needs. Facebook is one of the most efficient business networks which help people in discovering new channels.

If figures are representing its recognition, it can say that Facebook is the next big thing for aspirant in enterprisers. This well-liked social network site has more than 200 million people addicted to it. It stood as the second largest website on the internet. Reasonably, it is a networking hub which has found support from all over the world.

Previously, for business purpose entrepreneurs were unconvinced to get an account in social networking site. Their concern was how a social networking site would help people in meeting their old pals and acquaintances for any kind of reason.

However, it was cleared that Facebook plays a vital role for changing the way we do business. Now business owners are realizing that enhancing their online presence is a major concern which cannot be neglected and it has also been cleared that only Facebook helps you in achieving this target.

Fascinatingly, Facebook stood at first place among its challengers in tapping the business opportunities which exists in the dot com world. Introducing several features that are endorsing businesses to market themselves, they are using Facebook as a source. As this becomes an interactive forum, Facebook users are becoming fans of the products and companies.

Actually, people are scattering good words about the products they are using making it easier for the companies to market their products. Hence, it is essential that for internet marketing you can make use of the social media network, Facebook.

Due to rapid modernization over the network, it is essential that companies overlook more chances as such can turn upbeat. Bebo and LinkedIn are releasing their individual developers and APIs as well.

Conclusion

Now that you are aware of the many wonders of the Facebook tools, why not get started. Through this tool there is so much that you can do. Make money, expand your business and even make friends.

It's the perfect opportunity for you to revamp your business opportunities and change the way you perceive the world. There is so much to be done here. Working becomes fun; clients become friends and your experience. The idea is that you enjoy the most of both the worlds. So get started with your Facebook experience today and enjoy the wonders of this cool and generation Z website.

CHECK OUT BRIAN'S OTHER BOOKS

(his writings touch on over 400 different subjects.)

Hayward House
Publishing

1_rev copy copy.jpg · 1Untitled.jpg · 3.jpg · 4 copy copy.jpg · 5 copy copy.JPG · 6 copy copy.JPG · 7 copy copy.jpg · 8.jpg · 9.jpg

10 copy copy.jpg · 11 copy copy.JPG · 12 copy copy.JPG · 13.jpg · 14.jpg · 15 copy copy.jpg · 16 copy copy.jpg · 17 copy copy.jpg · 18.jpg · 19.jpg

20 copy copy.jpg · 21 copy copy.jpg · 22.jpg · 23 copy copy.jpg

Get The Whole Series

Works Cited

Berchie, Daniel. *Bible*. Cambridge Scholars Publishing, 2016.

Copeland, Kenneth. *Our Covenant with God*. Harrison House, 1999.

Copeland, Kenneth, and Gloria Copeland. *From Faith to Faith: Devotional : a Daily Guide to Victory*. Harrison House, 1999.

---. *Pursuit of His Presence: Daily Devotions to Strengthen Your Walk with God*. Kenneth Copeland Publications, 2012.

"Course Textbooks | W. W. Norton & Company." *Home | W. W. Norton & Company*, books.wwnorton.com/books/college-subject.aspx?id=4294983309.

The King James Study Bible: King James Version. Thomas Nelson Publishers, 2008.

Washington, Booker T, and William L. Andrews. *Up from Slavery: Authoritative Text, Contexts, and Composition History, Criticism*. Norton, 1996.

Winston, Bill. *Faith & the Marketplace*. 2016.

---. *The Kingdom of God in You: Discover the Greatness of God's Power Within*. Harrison House, 2010.

---. *The Law of Confession: Revolutionize Your Life and Rewrite Your Future with the Power of Words*. Harrison House, 2009.

---. *Training for Reigning: Releasing the Power of Your Potential*. HigherLife Development Services, 2011.

---. *Transform Your Thinking, Transform Your Life: Radically Change Your Thoughts, Your World, and Your Destiny*. Harrison House, 2008.

World's Concordance to the Holy Bible: King James Version. World Pub. Co, 1969.

https://www.biblegateway.com/quicksearch/?quicksearch=jehovah&qs_version=KJV

http://biblehub.com/mark/4-38.htm

http://biblereasons.com/fishing/

https://www.google.com/search?q=all+equipment+needed+to+fish&ie=utf-8&oe=utf-8&aq=t&q=all+equipment+needed+to+fish&ie=utf-8&oe=utf-8&aq=t&channel=fflb&q=all+equipment+needed+to+fish&ie=utf-8&oe=utf-8&aq=t&channel=rcs

http://www.knowyourphrase.com/phrase-meanings/Give-a-Man-a-Fish.html

http://www.christianbiblereference.org/faq_faith.htm

https://bible.knowing-jesus.com/words/Fish-hook

https://bible.knowing-jesus.com/topics/Fishes

https://www.allaboutgod.com/jesus-fish.htm

http://biblehub.com/matthew/4-4.htm

http://www.biblemeanings.info/Words/Animal/Fishes.htm

http://www.patheos.com/blogs/christiancrier/2015/07/17/what-does-water-represent-in-the-bible-a-christian-study/

https://www.copyscape.com/prosearch.php

https://www.biblegateway.com/quicksearch/?quicksearch=jehovah&qs_version=KJV

http://biblehub.com/mark/4-38.htm

http://biblereasons.com/fishing/

http://www.knowyourphrase.com/phrase-meanings/Give-a-Man-a-Fish.html

http://www.christianbiblereference.org/faq_faith.htm

https://bible.knowing-jesus.com/words/Fish-hook

https://bible.knowing-jesus.com/topics/Fishes

https://www.google.com/search?q=faith+confessions+about+faith&ie=utf-8&oe=utf-8&aq=t&q=faith+confessions+about+faith&ie=utf-8&oe=utf-8&aq=t&channel=fflb&q=faith+confessions+about+faith&ie=utf-8&oe=utf-8&aq=t&channel=rcs

http://www.kcm.org/real-help/faith/speak/faith-confessions

chrome-

extension://oemmndcbldboiebfnladdacbdfmadadm/https://www.billwinston.org/uploadedFiles/

Faith%20Confession.pdf

http://biblehub.com/matthew/4-4.htm

http://www.biblemeanings.info/Words/Animal/Fishes.htm

http://www.patheos.com/blogs/christiancrier/2015/07/17/what-does-water-represent-in-the-

bible-a-christian-study/

https://www.biblegateway.com/passage/?search=2+Corinthians+5%3A7&version=NKJV

chrome://bookmarks/

https://mail.google.com/mail/mu/mp/619/#tl/priority/%5Esmartlabel_personal

Hayward House
Publishing

Hayward House
Publishing

www.ingramcontent.com/pod-product-compliance
Lightning Source LLC
Chambersburg PA
CBHW081649220526
45468CB00009B/2595

9781981560820